D1488815

How To Create
The Organisational
Culture You Want

RALPH MAYHEW

ISBN-10: 1535335416
ISBN-13: 978-1535335416

DEDICATION

This book is dedicated to Azaria and Hamish:
you are forever enriching the culture of our lives.
We love you.

CONTENTS

SPECIAL THANKS

To Lyndal – you are my constant source of encouragement and doing what you do in our lives enables me to do all of this.

To all the people I've led and all the organisations I've led in – you have taught me so much about culture.

To my editor Andrew Hartwig – you are so patient and encouraging and I've gained much from your great insights.

To Maureen Oldfield – you are an incredible proof reader who only makes my work better.

To Susan Crittall – your wisdom in making sure that what I'm saying and how I'm leading is helpful and healthy, both in this book and in my life, is such a blessing.

To Matthew McNamee – your willingness to trial this work and provide me with feedback has been invaluable, as is your friendship.

To the leaders I lead with at Newlife Uniting Church – you are all so gifted and I am constantly blessed to gain from your thinking.

To those of you who fed back, asked questions, and added to my thinking with this material – you've all contributed to the health of many other organisations.

INTRODUCTION

Culture has the power to stop vision in its tracks, sabotage strategy and derail the intentions of incredible leaders. Understanding the power of culture and how it can be a huge asset is vital to effective leadership and producing great churches, organisations and businesses.

In reading this book you will learn what culture is and how to identify it. You will be equipped to challenge, shape and change it, so that people's needs are met and healthy organisations are experienced. Culture has rules to abide by and principles to obey, and as a leader you need to understand this in order to bring healthy change to work environments, teams, customer experiences and your own reputation. Culture is also determined by those within your organisation and the multitude of interactions on every level of an organisation.

Therefore I invite you to join me over the next few pages as we explore the relationship between leadership and culture, so that we might become skilled in using them to the advantage of the causes we have given ourselves to.

WHERE WE START THIS CONVERSATION

In the interest of transparency you need to know that I am a pastor. I have led people over the last 20 years in a vast array of different environments, structures and settings, both in the church and in business. I also have two Bachelors Degrees and a Masters Degree in Leadership, enabling me to offer informed ideas on culture and leadership. I spend much of my current time living in the realities I write about. I have found the learning I receive from these realities and the accompanying research I am engaged in, also powerfully applies to the business and social sector worlds, not just the church.

Many business-minded friends, who have worked in the marketplace or other social settings, have validated the reflections I include in this book and the conclusions you are about to benefit from. While my references are mostly drawn from church related situations, they have been deemed just as valid in any setting where people come together to achieve.

I present these thoughts to you in the hope that regardless of your pursuit and cultural setting you will benefit from them. May you use them to ensure a more enjoyable and productive experience for yourself and your people, doing the things you love and furthering the cause you serve.

For a free tool to help you evaluate the cultural health of your organisation and improve it, go to www.ralphmayhew.com/culture-tool.

1

WHAT IS CULTURE?

Culture is all about relationships. As a leader you will only find effectiveness if you can relate to those you are leading and helping to move forward. The better you become at understanding people, the more proficient you will become at shaping culture.

Culture only happens where there are people, it is the product of those people relating to each other. Shaping culture is about valuing and loving people, about wanting what is best for those people. It is about using what you know, and the influence you have attained through relationships to create environments in which those people can thrive.

You will undoubtedly encounter some people who are not as keen to relate to you as you are to them, you will have to lead those who may take a long time to trust you, if at all. You will come across people who feel like they are trying to sabotage you or your efforts. Changing culture is painful, but remember that those who you encounter, who may hurt you, slow you down, want you to fail, or are so fearful that they will do anything to stop you, they are the people you are to love. You are their leader.

Loving everyone you lead is not easy, but it is necessary if you are to truly embrace the trust people have given to the leadership position you now hold. This book will help you to navigate these tensions and offer you many skills and tools to be able to serve effectively those you lead, while creating a culture that is life giving for all. Let's start by addressing the mechanics of leadership.

There are many leadership phrases and words and they can easily cause confusion. To ensure we all start in the same place when thinking about the topic of culture, I have provided a brief summary of what each word means in the context in which I will use them:

Mission is the essence of what an organisation wants to achieve, explained in a single sentence.

Vision is the unique and inspired picture, which describes what the future can look like if the mission is pursued.

Strategy is the expression and plan of how the organisation intends to fulfill its vision.

Goals are the steps which need to be taken in a strategy to realise the vision.

Values are the agreed upon (but not always verbalized) behaviours, which determine the expression of an environment.

Culture is the feel, vibe and culmination of everything that the environment is.

Culture sits as the foundation upon which all organisations grow. It is the basis for success in one's mission, vision, strategy, goals and values. Think of it like an incubation system, which if calibrated correctly, can enable the healthy growth of whatever is in the incubation system. If calibrated incorrectly, however, just as quickly things will diminish and eventually die. That incubation system is culture. Calibrate your culture correctly and healthy growth will happen.

Culture is the vibe and feel of an establishment. It's the giver of your first impressions and is derived from the habits of a society or community of people. It impacts and determines your interactions. It's the informant of how you feel and the revelation of values at work. Culture is an organisation's subconscious.

We all live in a culture. Today alone, you would have engaged in multiple cultures if you ventured outside your front door, turned on the television or radio, called a friend or engaged with your family.

Culture is created when two or more people interact. Sometimes it's fleeting, empty and non identifiable but it can be riveting, disturbing, exciting, surprising, wholesome or toxic.

Culture is the expression of values that two or more parties bring to an interaction. When those values collide with each other and create friction, a culture is born. You cannot be a culture by yourself. Interact with anyone else and a culture begins to emerge, which can quickly vanish, or grow into something very powerful.

Culture can always be named. It may be difficult at times, but everything about culture can be identified. If someone refuses to do the hard work of identifying the culture, it becomes easy for them to blame the culture itself. They can be heard saying things like *'The culture just has a bad feel to it.'* While this might be true, it is an excuse for not addressing the real work required of leaders. It is possible and necessary to identify what your organisational culture is. Without the diligent application of such work, sustainable organisational health will be elusive.

As I have trialed this work in a number of industries, including education and technology firms, an interesting realisation has come to light. Many of the people working in these places with great leaders, have no understanding about what culture is. When asked to engage in conversation about this material, or to access the cultural health of their organisation they have stared back with blank faces.

If you are a leader, understanding culture is essential, but it may well be that the people you lead or manage have no understanding of what culture is, what the word means or how it works. Being aware of this better equips you to first educate your people, ensuring everyone's understanding is equal, before leading people through a process of cultural evaluation and then change. With the Measure Your Cultural Health Tool, you will also find a one page cheat sheet you can give to your people, so that they can easily and quickly understand the fundamentals of culture.

Culture is the measurable expression of a multitude of elements coming together to create how an environment is experienced by others.

Let's break this down:

Measurable – Culture can be measured and because it can be measured it can be strategically and intentionally changed.

Expression – Culture is the expression of something else; the shared assumptions, values, and beliefs that determine what the expression (or culture) looks like.

Multitude of elements – There are many intangible factors that when they converge in a specific environment, shape what the environment looks like.

Environment – Every culture is held in an environment. An environment is a space where people come together.

Experienced by others – Culture is best gauged by the experience of others. The greater the experience others have of your culture, the stronger the connection between your shared assumptions, values and beliefs, becomes.

In light of this, for a basic and assessable working definition we're using:

Organisational culture = shared assumptions, values, and beliefs, which determine how we behave.

Organisational culture is:

The things we together *assume* to be right and the way things should be.

The *values* we all agree on and want to see represent our organisation.

The *beliefs* we all share and have in common regarding our organisation and its goods or service.

These shared assumptions, values, and beliefs have a strong influence on the people in the organisation and dictate how they interact with customers and staff, how they dress, act, behave, treat each other, respond to issues and in general perform their jobs.

Organisational culture is the shared assumptions, values, and beliefs, which determine how we behave. This is the definition that will enable our thinking on this subject to be helpful. If you ever get lost in thinking about culture, just return to this idea and proceed forward again.

2

HOW DO WE WORK OUT WHAT OUR CULTURE IS?

Before we set about identifying or changing our culture, we must first be able to identify what it is. Culture is established through channels which constantly flow into and shape an organisation. These channels are Stories, Behaviours, Justifications, Consequences, Interactions and Feelings held by the people who are present in your organisation:

Stories

Stories are what birth a culture. What are the stories people recall, good and bad? These situations and experiences have shaped the culture in which you now exist. Just as a story of pain doesn't mean a poor culture, equally a story of joy and success may not result in a healthy culture. Knowing your cultural stories is a powerful tool you can use in affecting the culture. By knowing the stories you know the history, and by knowing the history you can create a healthy future.

Behaviours

People's behaviour contributes to culture. If an organisation has a culture of listening, it's because people are slow to speak and quick to receive what's being said. If not, the reverse may be true. If the culture is not one of mutual respect, it's because people gossip, judge and betray confidences. If the culture is one of transparency, it's because people behave with integrity, openness and honesty. The behaviour of people determines what the culture is and can change what a culture will be.

Justifications

In every organisation reasons exist for every decision that is made. Those reasons are clear signposts to what is most important to the organisation. Everything that happens in your organisation happens for a reason and the reason *why* something happens will point to the true culture. To discover it, start asking why different decisions are being made, or why certain instructions are being given. If it's not wise to offer the boss a suggestion of how the organisation might be improved, then there is a culture of 'what the boss says goes.'

Consequences

When you examine the results of decisions made, powerful cultural forces are revealed. Every decision is made because of a culture and every decision contributes to a culture. What consequences do you see that point to an aspect of culture? If the volunteerism in your organisation is very low (a consequence), what sort of leader is leading? If The Leader is strong and competent, but has high control issues, and needs everything to be done right or not at all, then a cultural truth begins to emerge. If there is no creativity expressed at any level of the organisation, except from The Leader, then perhaps the way decisions are made and the way brainstorming occurs is causing this.

Interactions

The way people interact with each other and with customers is a significant cultural indicator. The manner in which people talk about and to others, often reveals what the culture is like. Examine these interactions and you'll see the insecurity, fears, pain, care, priorities and dreams of the people and the organisation. Is there a shared mutual respect or is the opposite true?

Feeling

Every organisation has a *feel* to it, some by accident, and the wise ones by intention. Pixar has a very intentional feel to it, because the building was designed with meticulous intent by Steve Jobs to create a certain *feel*. McDonalds has a feel to it, just like a five star restaurant does. Many things shape the *feel* of an organisation (which we'll cover later on) and being aware of them helps you identify what the culture is.

There are some helpful questions you can ask of your organisation, which will help you understand what forces are shaping your culture. These include:

- What do I see when I look around?
- What do I hear when people are speaking?
- What do I feel, what is the vibe of the place?

- What is evoked in me when I interact with people or hear of decisions made?
- What does this place remind me of?
- What am I being told, even when no one is speaking?
- What is the emotional response I have to experiencing this organisation?

A great experiment to practice reading and identifying culture, is to evaluate your most recent shopping experience. Go back there in your head and run through the questions above. By the end of the exercise you should be clear on what the culture of not only that shop is, but also the brand they represent.

The same is true for a church, ministry, business, community group, group of friends, social movement, family, etc. These questions strip back what the culture of a place is. If you're still unsure, walk through the place when people are actively engaged there, and ask these questions, observing intently the signs you see, the interactions occurring, what people are wearing, the colours you're presented with, the smells and sounds you detect, the space (or lack thereof) surrounding you. All of these things speak to the culture, which reveals the experience those in the culture are having.

This is why organisational culture is so important. Culture shapes people and their experience. As leaders, we are responsible for those people and their experience. To ensure that they are healthy and enjoying their experience, we must make sure the culture is healthy and productive.

3

WHAT CULTURE DO YOU WANT?

"Healthy cultures never happen by accident. They are a
product of what you create and what you allow."
– Craig Groeschel

Culture is not only formed by the actions you take, but
also the actions you don't take. That difficult conversation
you've been avoiding can threaten culture, that hard
strategic issue you've been procrastinating about will be
impacting your culture. While much of this book is about
creating a healthy culture, the powerful force lurking in the
shadows waiting to sabotage our culture needs to be
addressed, avoidance. What you avoid is the very thing
that will grow more powerful the longer you avoid it. If
you avoid addressing poor value alignment or culture
defeating attitudes, then those things will gradually take
over and become the culture. Be aware of what you create
but also what you allow.

Often leaders don't want the culture they have but they are
not clear on what they do want. Becoming clear on the

culture you want is absolutely essential if you want to change it.

Culture is the shared assumptions, values, and beliefs which determine how we behave. If values are the behaviours which determine what this environment looks like, then culture is shaped by identifying what your values need to be, developing them and getting everyone to own them. Achieving this can be difficult, as it is a time consuming task, but without it, all your attempts to truly change the culture will be futile.

A helpful tool, which will equip you to begin thinking this way is the Measure Your Cultural Health Tool, which can be downloaded at www.ralphmayhew.com/culture-tool. By doing this helpful assessment of your organisation you'll quickly see what needs attention, and then be shown what steps you need to take.

As a leader, before you embark on cultural change you have to be clear on what you want things to look like when you're done. Don't just look at the negative aspects of your culture and think 'I don't want people to gossip anymore', or 'I don't want people turning up late to meetings anymore.' Instead, identify what a positive culture looks like: where gossip is forbidden or where people are excited to get to meetings on time. Having a clear picture in your head is essential to developing a healthy culture.

Two thousand years ago a man lived who out of obscurity created a movement that was to impact the world, and has for every generation since. His name was Jesus and he was a master at creating culture and enabling people to participate in this new culture.

He called this idea the Kingdom of God. He claimed that it was how things were meant to be in accordance with how God had initially created the world. This Kingdom came with a clearly defined culture, which was extremely counter to the culture of the day. Those who dared to follow him were invited to adopt this culture as He had a very clear idea of what it was and how it worked. This resulted in a counter-cultural movement which showed people the way to live to a different rhythm.

At the beginning of the New Testament, the part of the Bible which specifically explores Jesus' human life and the impact He had, we hear Jesus speak about this culture. It's in what has become known as the Beatitudes which were part of his sermon on the mount. The gospel of Matthew says, 'Now when Jesus saw the crowds, he went up on a mountainside and sat down. His disciples came to him, and he began to teach them.' He then spoke eight sentences that paint a picture of kingdom culture. (Matthew 5:1-12)

When Jesus said, "Blessed are the poor in spirit, for theirs is the Kingdom of Heaven," He is using an Old Testament root word that ties 'poor' to humble. Those who worshipped God were known as 'poor in spirit' or 'humble in spirit' because they recognised exactly who they were before God. They recognized they were in need so they chose to let God take the lead in their lives. Kingdom culture is about God leading the leader first, so that the leaders might offer their leadership to their people.

When Jesus said, "Blessed are those who mourn, for they will be comforted," He was exposing the heart of the

Kingdom. All believers should feel grief when they consider all that sin has taken away. Sin should shock us at the horrific offence it is to God, both the sin we commit and the sins that steal others from God. The comforting is in the Grace, not a warm grandmotherly cuddle, but the power God has claimed over sin. Sin will not have the last word. Kingdom culture is about God offering Grace to disempower sin through the lives of those who love Him.

When Jesus said, "Blessed are the meek, for they will inherit the earth," He was speaking of discipline, resilience and security. D.A. Carson says "Meekness is a controlled desire to see other's interests advance ahead of one's own." This perspective on life allows a person to let go of all they might otherwise strive to hold onto. An Anonymous Leader is a meek leader. The inheritance spoken of is reminiscent of God's promise to the Israelites that they will have a home, security and land to call their own. Kingdom culture is about God's generosity taking care of everyone who prefers everyone else.

When Jesus said "Blessed are those who hunger and thirst for righteousness, for they will be filled," He was calling those who realised they could not continue to live without righteousness, to become right with God. In hungering and thirsting for such things a person yearns to conform to God's will. In so doing, their famished soul is met by God's willingness to fill them. Kingdom culture is about God's will completely defining a person to the point of utter dependence on God.

When Jesus said, "Blessed are the merciful, for they will be shown mercy," He was wanting the warmth of the people's hearts to reach out to those who have less, who are on the margins, who are hated by society, or lonely, and meet them with compassion and kindness. In saying this Jesus wants His hearers to see how undeserving they are of God's mercy. In understanding this they are able to both give and receive mercy. Kingdom culture is about God's compassion and kindness becoming the first action taken, empowered because of God's initiated action toward his creation already.

When Jesus said, "Blessed are the pure in heart, for they will see God," He was impressing upon all of his listeners that a pure heart was the most essential and indispensable prerequisite for relating to God. Purity is important because the Kingdom of God is a pure Kingdom, led by a holy and pure King. It is only through purity that people can encounter God. Kingdom culture is about God's purity defining people's hearts and enabling them to see Him.

When Jesus said, "Blessed are the peacemakers, for they will be called children of God," He was calling them to walk in His footsteps, both physically for those who walked with Him and spiritually for those who would follow Him later. Jesus was the epitome of peacemaking - not peacekeeping - first and foremost by creating peace between people and God. Peacemaking is to permeate every aspect of people's lives, words and actions. In living as such they become children of God, referring to the culturally relevant dynamic where the father's offspring exhibits the character strengths of their father.

As peace increases in a person's life, so does the character of God in their beings. Kingdom culture is about God's character defining all that His people are.

Jesus said, "Blessed are those who are persecuted because of righteousness, for theirs is the Kingdom of Heaven." To be defined by righteousness is to be determined to live as God wills a person to live. This will bring opposition as it works itself out in a person's life. It is the righteousness in a person's life that causes social, political and religious friction, as the things of God are embodied and come to affect the things of this world. Kingdom culture is about God's righteousness affecting the state of this world through the lives of those who follow.

I expand on the implications of these in my book The Anonymous Leader, chapter 6. For now they act as a helpful picture, enabling you to think about how your culture needs to be different from what it currently is.

4

THE TEN RULES OF CULTURE

Like nearly everything in our universe, culture is governed by rules. Not the kind of rules you can break, but the kind that break you if you don't pay attention to them. Many leaders have grown frustrated by their culture because they've not understood the rules culture is required to operate by. By understanding these rules, we can be greatly equipped to use them to our advantage.

1. Only The Leader can determine what the culture is.

If you are not The Leader (Boss, CEO, Head Honcho), you do not have the final say on what the culture of your organisation looks like. Only The Leader does. If you are that person, you are the determining factor. Shocking, isn't it? But it's true. The Leader is the one who has the greatest influence, power and permission in an organisation, so they set the culture. If The Leader isn't completely committed to an aspect of cultural health it will never prevail. The Leader, which may be you, needs to realise that they are the cultural thermostat of your organisation.

2. You can determine the culture below you, but not above.

If you are not The Leader, you cannot determine what the culture is upwards, you can only determine what it is downwards. As a leader you are responsible for this. You may at times wish to blame The Leader when the culture below you is skewed, but you have the responsibility to shape the culture below you to what you feel is healthy. If your Leader is lazy and unproductive, you cannot make him or her more engaged, but you can certainly make clear to those you lead that you won't tolerate this behaviour in them. You can determine what the culture under your leadership will be like. If your Leader is unpredictable in his or her praise and punishment, leaving you constantly doubting what they want and need, you can arrest those same traits in your leadership and create a culture in your department that is one of trust and security.

3.   Regardless of your position,   you can affect   all culture.

Everyone is part of a culture; therefore, everyone can affect it. If there is enough groundswell, or strategic approach, those who are not The Leader, can sway The Leader towards a desired culture. The Leader, however, is the one responsible for the culture in an organisation and will determine its ability to be sustained across the whole. This means you can talk to The Leader about behaviours you see in him or her that you feel are culture killers. You can bring to their awareness unhealthy cultures present in your organisation. You can petition your Leader and challenge them and maybe you'll even sway them. You can convince those leading alongside you to adopt the same cultural values and live them out. What you can't do is ensure that this happens throughout the entire organisation. Only The Leader can do that.

4. Culture eats strategy for breakfast.

Management guru, Peter Drucker said it, and reality reinforces it, 'Culture eats everything for breakfast.' This includes vision, mission, motivation, momentum, values and goals. You can have the strongest strategy, clearest vision and most compelling goals, but a poor culture will sabotage you every time. Why? Because culture is your people, and the execution of your vision, mission, goals and strategy are only ever as good as your people. The only thing that can withstand a culture is a strong intentional leader. Don't slip into the myth that culture cannot be changed. It may take time but it can be changed, you just need to be smarter than it.

5. People will decide on everything else, based on your culture.

We love certain experiences because of the culture. That culture is shaped by the expression of values championed by the people involved. People come to our church and say, 'this feels like home'. Then they start to find out what we stand for and either accept or struggle with it, but they do so after they feel like they belong. Culture helps people belong, it's what causes them to think they're *home*. A healthy culture has the power to not only draw people in but also win them to your vision and beliefs, even if they don't initially agree with them. When people don't agree with the culture; perhaps they don't like it, or are uncomfortable with it, initially they will establish a counter-cultural movement. They will rebel against the current culture and recruit others to join them. As a leader this feels very threatening, but culture, if it is strong enough, pushes out those who do not like it. Culture is what enables a person to remain in a place. It is also what forces people to depart from organisations they don't wish to compliment. Be careful how much energy you exert trying to convince those counter-culturalists to re-adopt your culture. Instead continue to work at strengthening your healthy culture and everything else will take care of itself.

6. Culture is the most important, yet invisible force in your organisation.

Culture is invisible, but everyone can see it and everyone can feel it. As a leader, culture cultivation has to be your primary goal. It needs to be constantly on your radar and something you are consistently aware of. Everyone knows what your culture is, even if they cannot articulate it. People will make significant life decisions based on your culture, so you need to be constantly and effectively cultivating it.

7. You can't fake culture.

It can be easy to spend lots of time and energy trying to convince others what your culture is and isn't. This is wasting resources, because they already know what your culture is. Convincing them it's different is investing in a fake culture. Culture just is! Call it what you like, but at the end of the day what your culture is, is what people will experience. Language shapes culture (more on that soon), but you lose people to your cause if you tell them that your culture is something it isn't. Be aspirational as you speak about what you want your culture to be, but ensure people realise you're not blind to the current realities and limitations of your culture.

8. Culture repeats.

Repetition is what makes something cultural – consistently present, constantly repeating the same thing over and over. Call it the habits of a society. The only way to intercept this is to create a different pattern which stands opposed to a culture's rhythm and continue it long enough until it becomes a viable and then attractive option for those embedded in the current culture. The best way to break a habit is to create a new and healthy reward and then exploit the habit-trigger to direct your attention in a new way. Charles Duhigg's book the Power of Habit is brilliant if you want to delve deeper into this world of thought. The same strategy can be used with culture. By setting up a different expectation to the current culture you can then reward people for choosing to adopt this new culture. Once you've rewarded the behaviours which reinforce your desired culture consistently, you can then enable everyone to permanently invest in the new culture their behaviour has created.

9. Language sets culture.

The language people use, from the words, to the phrases, to the sentences, to the way they are all said, shapes the culture of a group of people. If The Leader speaks about the same things often enough those closest to them will start to unknowingly do the same and so gradually an entire organisation is shaped. Be clear and intentional with language. What are the phrases you constantly find yourself reverting back to again and again? They are culture shaping words. What are the concepts you always seem to circle around when talking about vision or strategy or helping people problem solve? This language is powerfully cultural.

10. Culture will decline in health if not intentionally and consistently kept healthy.

Everything, if left unattended will decay. Culture is no different. It will never stop being culture, but it will stop being healthy. Healthy culture can only be maintained by healthy leadership and a healthy pursuit of cultural excellence. Excellent leaders need to be constantly aligning culture with what they desire it to be, as it won't naturally self-align. This leadership doesn't need to be forceful or powerful, but it does need to represent the values everyone desires to experience in the culture.

5

THE CULTURE OF THE HEART

As a leader, the condition of your heart is the most powerful force in determining what the culture of your organisation will be like. As strange as it sounds, your heart has a culture. Its culture is shaped by the hurts, resentment and bitterness you still hold onto, the insecurities you have, the fears that command and direct you. Your heart's culture is also determined by what brings you joy, the way you understand and value people, the triumphs and wins you've had, the encouragement you've received, the rock solid convictions that guide you day to day, the attitudes you adopt and foster. Your worldview is also a very powerful factor in shaping the culture of your heart.

The heart is the epicentre of culture when it interacts with the expression of another's heart. In many ways, the stronger heart determines what the culture will look like. Your heart is what determines the success of your culture building endeavours and the heart of your organisation determines the health of your business. If there are others whose heart's desires oppose yours, then you have a battle on your hands.

If you're wondering how you begin to identify what the culture of your heart is, you can use the same grid we looked at in chapter 2.

To help you adopt the ideas expressed in that chapter, these questions should help:

- What do I see in me that is not healthy?
- What in me wants to find a joyful constant expression?
- What was I made to do and am I doing that?
- What do I hear myself saying to myself?
- What do I feel about the organisation I am leading?
- What is evoked in me when I think of the decisions we've made?
- What stories, conversations, encouragement or conflicts do I frequently revisit in my thoughts?
- What am I being told by myself about the problems our culture has?
- What do I feel in my heart toward everything else?

The simple act of regularly asking and answering these questions will increase your awareness about the culture of your heart. It will empower you to address inconsistencies and position yourself as the best leader you can be.

You need to be self-aware as a leader so that you can see the impact you are having on others. If you can develop the skill of self-awareness then you will be in a far greater position to powerfully affect the lives of others in positive ways. One way to advance the discipline of self awareness is to ensure you take time to reflect.

A simple framework you could use is to take 15 minutes each day to reflect on what happened in the previous day, how you reacted to it and why you reacted in the way you did. Developing a discipline such as this will enable you to gain a far more accurate and informed picture of yourself. As you do this you will find that you become more sensitive to the nuances of culture and more empowered to bring change where it is needed.

Shifting an unhealthy culture to a healthy culture always passes through the cultural filter of our hearts. It will determine how we look at things. What appears to be pessimistic or optimistic, bad and good, unhealthy and healthy, will be determined by the condition of your heart. If you align your heart with what is healthy, you will be able to see the accurate condition of things and be able to respond.

Your heart, and its condition or culture, will ultimately determine the cultural state of your organization. Regardless, if you are The Leader or a leader, the condition of your heart makes a huge difference to any culture you are in.

6

8 STEPS TO CHANGE
A CULTURE SLOWLY?

Framework 1: Slow Incremental Change

How do you change culture? This is one of the greatest questions a leader is required to answer. Great leaders will create great cultures. It's a sign of great leadership.

Culture is constantly changing, because the elements and people who generate culture constantly shift, change and adapt. When an organisation grows, culture will naturally shift if it is not constantly being anchored to what a leader desires. When people leave an organisation, some of the culture goes with them, as they are contributors to it. When there is conflict in an organisation the culture can fracture. When outside forces which affect an organisation increase or decrease, the culture can be powerfully moved. How an organisation responds to success or failure is a further force that can significantly shift culture.

Every leader has at their disposal two frameworks with which they can approach changing culture. This chapter is about facilitating slow incremental change. Slow incremental change is a powerful tool a leader can harness to bring change to a stubborn culture. Most effective cultural shift happens this way, where the power of culture gradually shifts to serve all the people who come (new recipients of your goods or service) as well as those who are already established recipients.

Let me provide you with an example of what I mean. We constantly want to see our church as a warm inviting environment where people feel at home. This is in contrast to the city in which we live, where the value placed on being in deep, selfless, loving, integral relationships is not high. For the last seven years, each week I've been speaking into this cultural dynamic and shaping it around hospitality, belonging and relationship. These days we hear numerous reports of people saying 'this place feels like home' or 'I love it here, I feel like I belong'. If you chip away at the opposing culture to that which you desire, little by little it will gradually disappear.

If you choose not to intentionally invest yourself in a key area of culture, it will decline to the lowest common denominator. Taking the example above, to not lead into that particular aspect of culture will result in it deteriorating into disengaged, loose, meaningless connections, leading to silos and cultural illness, similar to what many experience living in our city.

The same is true in an organisation. If you are concerned at the lack of energy your employees bring to their roles, leaving this unaddressed will not increase their motivation. It's likely your employees won't change if you tell them to be more energetic or engaged. It's a cultural issue in which you can either intervene with a sudden significant change or more realistically address with slow incremental change, gradually moving the culture from disengaged to energetic, exciting and fully engaged.

These 8 steps will guide you through how to create effective slow incremental change:

1. Examine what needs to change about your culture.

You'll need to identify what your culture is and where the gaps are, before you begin. We covered how to do this in chapter 5. Two helpful questions are:

1) What concerns you about your current culture?

2) What are people disgruntled with which compromises your vision?

These two questions are imperative to helping you work out what needs to happen.

2. Identify what is toxic and get rid of it.

Every culture has the potential for toxicity to breed and it must be arrested as soon as it's recognised. It may be a conversation you need to have with a person, a value you need to settle on and commit to, a dysfunctional program you need to shut down or a part of your organisation you need to amputate. Taking this seriously and acting swiftly is essential.

3. Ensure you are clear about why the change needs to happen.

Start by clearly articulating what is unhealthy about your culture and what the consequences of this are. These consequences then need to resonate with your followers. Your reason for cultural change cannot just be 'because it would make my life easier.' It has to be connected to something obvious that people already value. You need to help people see how uncomfortable and disadvantageous it will be to remain the same.

4. Work out who you need to first convince.

There are always a number of stakeholders who need convincing before you go public with your strategy. Write a list and be sure no one is forgotten as the repercussions of forgetting someone can be harsh. This step can be tedious and time consuming but it's invaluable as you start to shift the culture. Ask trustworthy companions who else should be on your list. Those people on your list are the ones for whom you need to work the hardest to bring up to speed and convince to trust and follow you.

5. Develop a strategy.

You need an effective strategy which negotiates all the foreseeable obstacles. It doesn't need to be a long-term plan, but it does need to be actionable and applicable to right now. Examples of this are that you might commit to using the same cultural language every time you speak with employees, you might seek to change the physical appearance and architecture, you might rebrand and possibly rename, you might introduce new cultural parameters of behaviors to be used in gatherings or meetings. The options are endless but be strategic about what you will focus on and then do it.

6. Identify the wins and celebrate them publicly.

How do you know you're getting the culture you want? Certain things will happen, and landmarks will be reached that require celebration. These are called wins. It is important that you identify what they look like, acknowledge and celebrate them. Doing so will encourage everyone that progress is being made. This means you need to work out how you will measure your success at changing the culture. As difficult as this is, it is essential to develop. The Measure Your Cultural Health Tool will help you to achieve this, as it outlines the components of a healthy culture.

7. Cultural change needs to affect everything.

For slow incremental change to prevail, it needs to seep into and affect everyone and everything in your organisation. This means across multiple departments, levels of authority and multiple sites. It needs to be shared with those recently joining your organisation as well as seasoned participants. Slow incremental change also needs to be owned by each member of staff or key volunteers throughout the entire organisation. Changes to culture need to filter into your systems and structures as well as your language and interactions. It really does need to filter into everything.

8. Consistently role model

Your ability to role model underpins the success of this cultural change. As The Leader, you need to consistently stick to and live out the change you are asking others to make. The quickest way to sabotage the culture you're trying to develop is failing to be flawless with the practice of it in your own life. If you want excellence in communication to increase, but you don't reply to texts and are late with email responses, the culture you desire will not emerge. Break culture once and people will forgive you, twice and they will doubt, three times they'll opt out of the desired culture and four (and more), they won't believe what you say about the culture you desire.

These eight insights will equip you to constantly lead your people toward healthy cultural change. Don't rush it, be intentional and you'll start to see significant progress in the life of your organisation.

7

7 STEPS TO CHANGE
A CULTURE QUICKLY?

Framework 2: Sudden Significant Change

Slow incremental change is not the only framework
available to a leader seeking to change the culture of their
organisation. This chapter is about the second framework,
creating sudden significant change. A leader can
intentionally use this framework, making the right
significant change at the right time, in a way which shocks,
inspires, surprises, motivates, moves or arrests people
across your organisation, having the affect of radically and
instantaneously shifting a culture. Sounds too good to be
true, doesn't it? But it isn't. It is however one of the
riskiest things you can do to your organisation.

When the horrific catastrophe we know as 9/11 occurred,
countless cultures all across the globe changed in an
instant. Fear invaded what was secure, leaving people
immediately more conscious of the fragility of life. People
felt less safe, and as a result their interaction with, and in
organisations, shifted significantly. It happened on a single
day and the effects of it are still shaping our world today.

The Sunday morning after 9/11, I preached in church, and it felt very different from the week before. Something had shifted in the same group who had gathered just a week earlier. While that sudden significant change was external, it significantly affected our organisation, as it did every organisation. No one could control the impact of such an event, once the attacks had happened. It was unavoidable, resulting in a significant cultural shift.

Just as this outside event powerfully shaped our inner cultural worlds, a leader can harness sudden significant change to their advantage to build a culture they desire. After 9/11, a great cultural doorway opened up for our culture to explore what vulnerability, fear and love looked like. Instead of remaining victim to this outside force, many used it to their benefit.

When our young adults church began with a handful of people, there was a great deal of debate surrounding the music. I share a lot more about the details surrounding this in chapter 9 of my book The Anonymous Leader. Basically, an unhealthy culture was developing, which was detracting from our central cause and purpose. No one seemed to be happy with the music, and it became a regular topic of debate every time we evaluated how healthy our church was. The music should never occupy this position.

To arrest our cultural decline and reshape it to serve our vision, I made the decision, with the agreement of everyone* to cancel all music in church. The veto lasted for 6 weeks, we explained why, continued to help people understand our course of action, drew their attention to what really was important (our mission), and when we reintroduced the music, people valued it in a different way. It held a different position in the life of our community.

100% buy in is rare. I was surprised everyone agreed to the idea. It's not necessary to have complete buy in, but it is important that you have key stakeholders on board, otherwise you run the risk of blowing everything up.

Sudden Significant Change isn't really about a product you offer, although it might be. We're not looking at how we change our customer's, or congregant's culture elsewhere, we're looking at how we change the environments within our organisations. We're talking about altering the way our people engage with each other and with our organisations. How we transform cultures that our people exist in outside of our organisations is for another book.

To suddenly and significantly change culture requires some essential elements to prevent your organisation from blowing up. These are as follows:

1. You need to be wise.

Effective Significant Sudden Change rises and falls on wisdom and timing. The timing has to be right and you need to be wise in your thinking about it. Surround yourself with others who are wise and glean from their thinking. Draw in people you trust who are wiser than you and listen to their opinions about what you're proposing. A great question to ask yourself is 'what would a wise leader do?' this question helps you think in ways you may not have already.

2. You need to understand timing.

Timing is essential to making great leadership decisions, yet leaders frequently overlook it. Timing is informed by how ready your people are, how prepared you are, the things going on inside your organisation, and the things outside of it. Make sure you take the time needed to execute your strategy at the most effective opportunity. Fast and soon are not necessarily always the best options

3. You need people who are hungry for change.

It's very important to have a core of people around you who acknowledge that cultural change needs to take place. If this is in place, then you are able to gradually spread an understanding among your people that the current culture is less than ideal. Without your people understanding why a Sudden Significant Change needs to occur, you run the risk of confusing, disorientating, isolating and then driving people away.

4. You need to have a strategy.

Much like I mentioned previously, you need a strategy. There is little value in jumping into huge change because you feel your organisation's culture needs it when you have no way of guiding people through it. People may follow you in, but if they don't feel like you know where it's going they'll be more likely to opt out. This doesn't mean you need to have all the answers, but it does mean you need to be alert, aware of what's happening and be at least one step ahead of your people. Doing this well will reassure your people the risk was worth it.

5. You need buy in from the key players.

John Kotter in his book Leading Change explains this in great detail. Your key supporters have to be aware of what you are thinking, what you are changing and why. If you fail to do this you risk ostracizing the very people you need to make the change effectively happen. If you secure their allegiance, your voice and your why will be carried by them throughout your organisation. If you fail to gain their loyalty you could be heading towards disaster.

6. You need to calm your doubts.

People will question your decision to bring Significant Sudden Change. They will ask you about it, they may not be supportive and they will cause you to doubt your wisdom and leadership. Don't be shy about the decision you've made. You have spent time weighing everything up. It's a good decision if you've followed all of these steps, so stick to what you've decided. You will inevitably second-guess your decision-making ability and find yourself wanting to change previous decisions. Recognise the doubt for what it is, file it away and push on. There may be wisdom in it you can mine later but don't need to listen to now.

7. Communicate. Communicate. Communicate.

You can't talk to your people enough during this time. Tell them why you're doing what you're doing and tell them again and again. Help them to talk about it, encourage questions and ask people how they are experiencing the change. The change you are ushering in is altering the way they engage with each other and with your organisation, so give them as much opportunity to process it as possible. Communication is your best friend. Don't stress about talking too much, you can guarantee there will be some who are there all the time and still don't get it.

These seven steps will allow you to navigate the treacherous path of Sudden Significant Change. Stick to them and change the right things at the right time and you should be able to lead your people effectively towards a healthy culture.

8

MAINTAINING CULTURE

Let's assume that you've taken what I've said seriously and begun to implement it. To completely change a culture can take up to seven years, depending on how you measure it. So while change is taking place, here are 12 important factors that will serve your leadership in maintaining focus and courage to ensure your desired culture is realized. These thoughts may also fill in some of the gaps you may have overlooked in the process.

1. Take action. Without taking action nothing will change, and there are always things to action where culture is concerned. Don't procrastinate and find excuses not to act. Your people need you to lead them.

2. Model the new culture. People need to see it in you consistently before they'll risk moving. Modeling won't cause them to follow you towards the culture, but it will prevent them from abandoning the culture. Modeling denies people the permission they look for to disengage.

3. Ensure you are diligent when it comes to doing the groundwork and research. As time consuming

as this may appear to be, it is essential if you are to be effective.

4. Check your motives and cultural direction against your moral compass and the organisation's values. It's important that everything is pointing in the same direction.

5. Ask how does your theology (thinking about God) or sociology/ anthropology (thinking about communities and people) inform your current and future culture? What you believe has to match what you want to see.

6. Always seek to get more people around the idea of culture than you currently have. Momentum comes when more people are more excited. The more the better.

7. Constantly build dissatisfaction and unacceptability with a current unhealthy culture. Do this while pointing people to what is possible in a healthy culture, and how that might be realised.

8. Compile a list of behaviours which, if followed will promote a healthy environment and grow healthy people. This list will act as a cultural blueprint for you.

9. Compile a list of unacceptable behaviours which if actioned, will not be acceptable or permitted in the new culture. Make this list known. If people know exactly what they are not allowed to do it will help increase your ability to hold them to account.

10. Make the expected behaviours applicable across your entire organisation. Every person needs to see that they can live out each cultural value.

11. Build relationships with key stakeholders, vocal parties, and people you want the culture to serve. The more intimate you are with their needs, hopes and pain, the more effective your cultural change process will be.

12. Ensure your key influencers are clear about everything, have bought into the ideas and are loyal to your vision.

There are other principles to keep in mind when it comes to maintaining culture, which I'd love to hear about. Cultivating an effective culture is a mix of art and science, and every leader in every organisation will do it slightly differently. If you can add to this thinking, I'd love to discuss it with you. You can email me at ralph@ralphmayhew.com.

9

CULTURE KILLERS AND FILLERS

CULTURE FULFILLERS

Leaders can do a great number of things to ensure their organisation fulfills the culture they want to see. Below are some essential elements every leader should be aiming to produce in his or her culture, as a result of their leadership.

1. The leader of a team who is good at keeping others accountable creates a culture of accountability. Accountability is the chain that holds the ship to its anchor. Accountability isn't about being angry, demanding or demeaning, it's often simple, gentle and with a smile. How you keep others accountable can be a huge asset or liability to your culture. As you seek to increase the health of your culture, you need to start holding others to account and encouraging them to do the same with those they influence. A culture of accountability is a powerful way to bring all of your culture into alignment.

2. A strong and healthy culture regulates itself with a communal set of values and standards which holds everyone to account. This means that once you've developed the culture you want and are implementing it, it will become its own regulating system, as enough people buy into it. To expedite the process, give people permission to hold each other to account. Help them understand what is culture-fulfilling behavior and praise it, and address culture-killing behavior.

3. Communicate, communicate, communicate the culture you want to see. I said it in chapter 7 and it needs to be said here again, communicate. Never tire of saying the same words, phrases and sentences, painting the same picture and calling people towards it. This needs to happen not just over days, weeks or even months, but over the course of the coming years. Everyone needs to speak the same language if culture is to shift and they will learn that language from their leader.

4. It is really important to give people practical handles to help them live out the culture. Be clear on what behaviours or actions are good and healthy and need to be repeated in increasing measure throughout the organisation. In the same manner be clear on behaviours and actions that are destructive to cultural health and won't be tolerated. Be as practical as you can and create opportunities for these new cultural values to be embedded in people's practice.

Be constantly on the look out for culture fulfillers and celebrate them. This is the fuel which enables your efforts to establish culture to become fruitful. Use these four principles in a myriad of ways to establish the new culture which will best serve your organisation.

CULTURE KILLERS

Leaders can do a great number of things to ensure that their organisation fulfills the culture they want to see. Below are some cautions every leader needs to heed, if they want to create a healthy culture.

1. If you fail to execute consistently towards the aspirational culture, you won't be successful at changing the culture. This goes further than modeling. It is about carefully executing every endeavor towards your commitment. Culture is consistent. What happens consistently becomes your culture. It's not enough for you to be living and breathing the culture. Every decision made needs to be executed with excellence, not forgotten or cast aside in the hope it will be forgotten. The Leader's responsibility is to ensure timely execution of pre-agreed commitments takes place.

2. Not addressing cultural violations when they occur gives them permission to breed. Your task as a leader is to identify cultural breaches as much as cultural wins. Elements of bad culture are like weeds in a garden. They invade, take over and then suffocate the healthy plants. Cultivating your culture is similar to what a gardener does; find and dig out those weeds. You cannot afford for cultural violations to remain, they will destroy your best attempts at moving your organisation to a healthy culture.

3. Double standards in a culture cause confusion for everyone. Treat everyone the same according to the agreed-upon values. If people see you treat some with favouritism or greater leniency than others, you will find a rapid decay in organisational integrity. Integrity is what gives your cultural change traction. You need to honour systems, structures and protocols everyone has agreed to and require others to do the same. Don't let those who have a more powerful position or more dominant personality live to a different standard than is expected of everyone else.

4. Align all decision-making with the cultural values you have developed. This can be the hardest aspect of change if you've got an already deeply ingrained culture you're trying to shift. All decisions being made and initiatives taken need to be driving the culture toward the state of health you want. Every decision made needs to be a small step toward fulfilling the vision. If it isn't, then it is a decision that shouldn't have been made.

In some respects culture is very robust, but in others it is very fragile. When changing culture, the new culture is untried and untested, and people by nature are approaching it with suspicion. Do all you can to eliminate the validation of their suspicion so they might be quick to adopt a healthy culture for the organisation they are a part of.

10

CONCLUSION

CONCLUSION

Culture comes from the word cultivation. Cultivation is slow healthy growth resulting in a fruitful harvest. The cultures we are in have enormous potential to become very fruitful. This only happens when the soil is tilled, the ground is enriched, watering is generous, sustenance is regular and the garden is stewarded by a wise and loving gardener.

You are the gardener of your culture. Care for it, protect it, feed it, guide it, weed it, encourage it and you will see wonderful things happen in the lives of your people and their families, and then in the life of your organisation and its recipients of your goods or service.

As I've taught on culture and asked leaders to identify cultural issues, a number of questions were raised which I felt required a little more attention than they have gotten in this book so far. It's by no means a comprehensive list, but it may be helpful to those of you wanting to dig a little deeper on more specific issues. If you have a question on this material or in addition to this material I would love to discuss it with you and invite you to email me at ralph@ralphmayhew.com.

For a free tool to help you evaluate the cultural health of your organisation and improve it, go to www.ralphmayhew.com/culture-tool.

11

APPENDIX Q&A

1. How do we work out what our culture is?

This is such an important question, so I created a tool to enable you to do this. It's called Measure Your Cultural Health Tool, and is available at www.ralphmayhew.com/culture-tool. This tool will help you evaluate your culture and in conjunction with this book, give you strategies to improve the culture of your organisation.

2. How do you handle negative/critical people in your culture without alienating them?

While the shadow side of our leadership may desire at

times to exclude a toxic or negative person from a culture, this is a last resort. An excellent culture, if upheld, will either change people to align with it or make it increasingly difficult for them to participate. This being said, people need to be won over.

Your principle calling as a leader is to win people over to a preferred future. The condition a person is in doesn't change your responsibility as their leader. You need to help this person find interest in what you are doing, stir their curiosity and then give them behavioural boundaries within which to operate. If people are interested in what you are doing you can then move them to full engagement. Without interest, they can gradually become disengaged, toxic or immovable.

If they become interested, it is essential that a person knows what they are allowed to do and not do. They need to know in very clear terms what your culture will tolerate and what will kill your culture. You then need to hold them accountable to these standards, encouraging them to remain within the boundaries you've set. I speak in far greater depth and detail about these boundaries, and how to maintain them, in chapter 6 of The Anonymous Leader.

3. How do you build a culture that values the different contributions people have to make?

A culture needs to be built with this premise in mind. Moving an established, yet unhealthy culture toward this ideal can be difficult. If the culture isn't already about this, then making it so can be a real challenge.

Cultures are made up of people. That's the essential ingredient to a culture. Each person has different things they bring to that culture, so enabling them to enrich it should be a leader's prerogative.

If your culture is one where you would like to value the different contributions of people, but those differences aren't currently being valued, then you need to invite people to step up and become active in what they can contribute. In order for this to be successful, your culture needs to be safe for a person to contribute. It may be that your culture needs to become a safe place first, so others will more freely desire to contribute to it.

4. How do you develop a cohesive culture that enables everyone (including volunteers) to bring their best, no matter their pay grade, so they can work effectively together?

The two values being championed in this question are excellence and team cohesion. Excellence is achieved with clear standards, high accountability and a desire from all to honour the importance of the cause.

Team Cohesion is about chemistry. It's easy to work effectively with people who:

- You like.
- Are of the same skill level.
- Have the same appreciation for excellence.
- Share a common value of accountability.
- Compliment your abilities.

- Are moving in the same direction with the same understanding.

These are the elements you need to foster as The Leader in the team or group of people you lead.

As a leader you need to be steering your culture toward excellence and team cohesion if you want everyone to bring their best and work effectively together. If your culture is about helping participants do this then the distinction between who is paid and who is a volunteer will fade away and be replaced with a team spirit of wanting to achieve the next great challenge together.

5. How do you help culture change to become outward (mission) focused rather than inward focused?

People are naturally inward looking. There are exceptions of course, but most people choose self-preservation before self-sacrifice. Keeping this in mind a leader needs to:

- Challenge people to look outward.
- Equip them with the skills and perspective to do so.
- Give them opportunities to experiment in a safe environment.
- Continue to communicate the importance of outward focus to the point that 'outward' is what defines us.
- Celebrate the wins.
- Address specifically the inward focused pockets that exist.

If an organisation can position itself to be primarily outward focused, it will see two results. It will attract those who hold the same outward focused values. It will also help those who are presently involved to become outward focused. If this doesn't happen then those who are unable will find the culture encouraging them to depart from the organisation.

6. What factors have the biggest influence in creating culture and/or changing it?

A well-intentioned leader has the greatest influence and impact on culture. Everything else will get swallowed up in an unhealthy culture's wake. A strong leader who refuses to be turned by the tide can redirect the tide if they are persistent enough. Of course clarity, values and execution are essential, but only if a well-intentioned leader is at the helm.

7. How does a large church keep a small church culture, and avoid breaking into cliques?

The same question can be asked of an organisation. Cliques emerge when people want to look after themselves at the expense of others. They become blind and deaf to everything and everyone else. Culture, if skillfully crafted, can sway a person, or a group of people, away from forming cliques by helping engagement with others to first be okay, then safe and then the norm.

Patrick Lencioni talks about this idea in Silos, Politics and Turf Wars. People group to what they value the most. They find safety in that space, refuse to move from it and can become quite disruptive. Your goal as a leader is to help them fall in love with the bigger picture more than their smaller picture. You need to move their loyalty from their little patch of land to the whole property.

In a small church it feels like a small patch of land (respectfully speaking), so competing silos rarely exist. Silos come with growth, but they don't need to be tolerated. Help the leaders of these cliques or silos to buy into and serve the bigger picture, and you'll find their allegiance to their small patch of land diminishes, when they realise they can have it all.

8. How do you create a culture from scratch?

A culture is formed by the coming together of two people. It is the result of their values, behaviours and ideologies rubbing up against each other, which produces culture. This means it is essential in the early stages of cultural development to have the right people in the mix. If one person out of ten is not on board with the desired culture this is a huge factor, whereas one person out of one hundred is not.

Desired culture begins in a very fragile state. There will always be culture, but it will not always be what you desire, so it needs to be nurtured to grow. You need to be strategic about it and police what is and isn't allowed. You need to lead those on board with intention and clarity. If you do this, and have a clear picture in your own mind of the culture you want to see developed, then the result should be a healthy organisation and an enrichment of the lives of those who follow you.

9. If you're not The Leader, should you attempt to use one of the frameworks mentioned in this book to change your culture?

These frameworks work at every level of an organisation. Any significant change in any part of an organisation will affect the whole. Therefore to be successful at this, you need to ensure that The Leader is happy with any changes to the culture which you want to make for your area or department. This may require some robust conversation and persistency, if you are to be successful in gaining permission. This outlines why having great relationships between all leaders in an organisation is imperative to healthy cultural change. It's both wise and adds much more enjoyment to your work.

Should you have any further questions on culture, I would be delighted to hear them and respond as best I can. You can email them to ralph@ralphmayhew.com.

OTHER BOOKS
BY RALPH MAYHEW

The Anonymous Leader: An Unambitious Pursuit of Influence.

www.theanonymousleader.com

The Anonymous Leader, by Ralph Mayhew, short listed for the Australian Christian Book of the Year Awards, is a refreshingly different angle on Christian Leadership, which calls you back to the core of what leadership is meant to be about.

Are you tired of leaders and leadership books that encourage self-serving principles? Are you searching for a way to lead change without changing yourself for the worse? Bestselling author Ralph Mayhew has an unconventional approach that will help you reclaim Jesus' heart for the people.

Too many leaders hijack themselves with a subconscious desire for fame and ambition. The true leader is much more anonymous, stewarding his or her platform so that the desires of God become the greatest priority for those who follow. *The Anonymous Leader* teaches gifted leaders like you to change your heart towards your people and lead with more humility.

In this book, you'll discover:

- How to make your leadership more about God to make greater things happen for your cause

- How to develop resilient leadership that lets you overcome any challenge

- How to see Christian leadership in a refreshing way, even if you would never call yourself "a leader"

- How to grasp the importance of values and culture to empower and guide more people

- How to love those you lead to maximize their impact, and much, much more!

Leadership is a God-given opportunity to influence others in a positive way. Using scripture and his own personal experience, Mayhew shares a new perspective on leadership that will ensure the greatness of your cause without encouraging your hungry ego. *The Anonymous Leader* teaches you to put your desire for acclaim aside for something much more empowering and fulfilling.

If you like practical, easy-to-read, and authentic nonfiction books with Biblical influence, then you'll love Mayhew's engaging guide to increasing your leadership capacity.

Buy *The Anonymous Leader* at to discover the true value of leadership today.
www.theanonymosuleader.com

ABOUT THE AUTHOR

RALPH MAYHEW IS married to Lyndal and together they have a two- year-old daughter, Azaria and a four-month-old son, Hamish. He is about to plant a church on the gold Coast, after serving for nine years as in an Associate capacity at Newlife Uniting Church, also on the Gold Coast, Australia (www.church.nu). Much of his ministry time is spent developing leaders, pastoring young adults, overseeing strategic church initiatives and supporting the Generational Ministries.

Ralph understands what it means to intentionally influence and empower people, enabling them to achieve their goals. Over the last 19 years he has led emerging, developing and seasoned leaders in and out of church settings. He has just completed his Masters in Christian Leadership and has two other bachelor degrees to his name (one in theology) as well as an Advanced Diploma in Ministry.

Ralph has been writing on the subject of Christian leadership for over ten years. He has an entrepreneurial spirit and loves to create – and encourage those who are doing the same. He loves people and lives to see them fulfill their God-given potential.

CPSIA information can be obtained
at www.ICGtesting.com
Printed in the USA
FFHW011324051118
49299402-53513FF

9 780994 630391